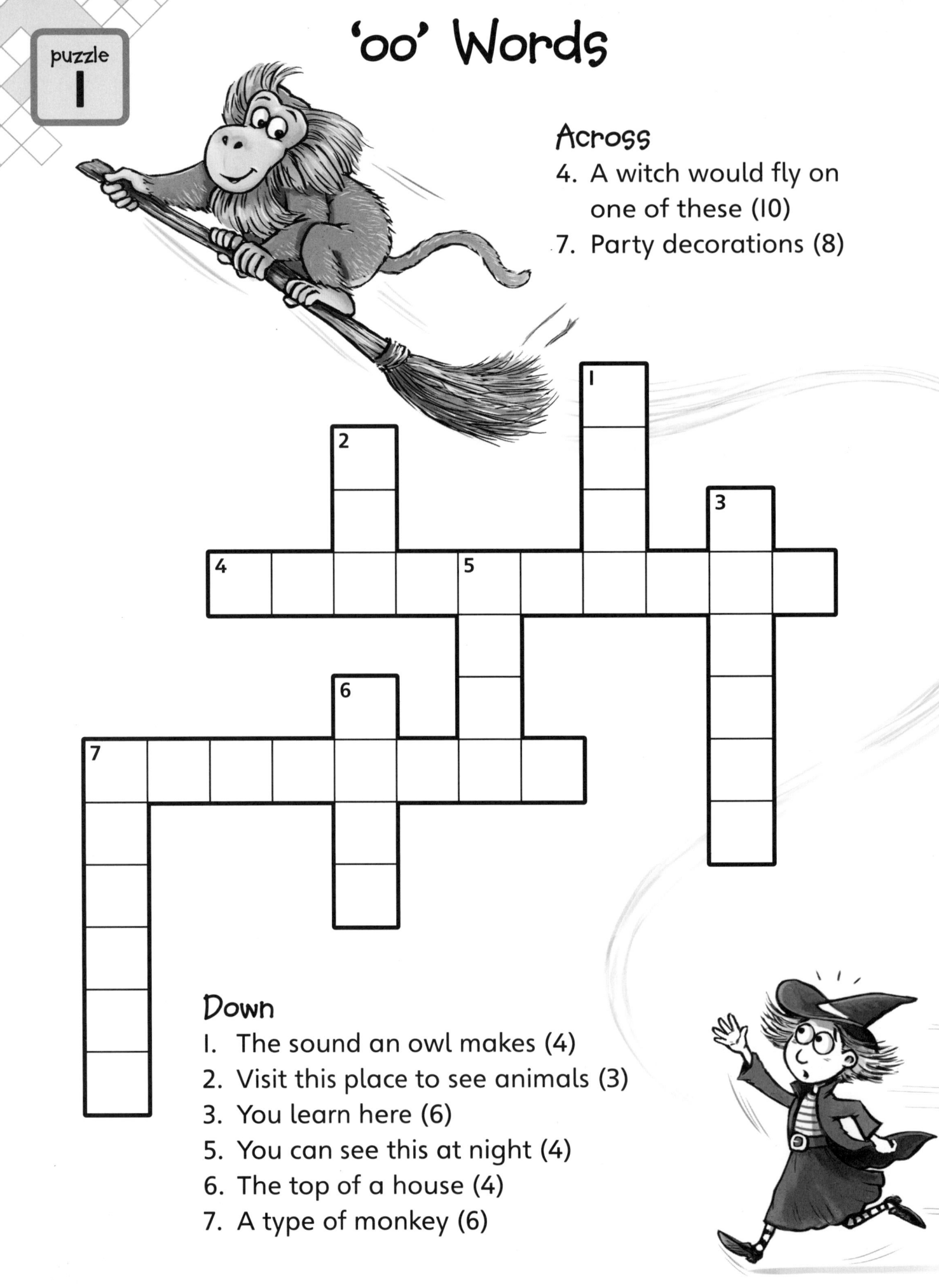

'oo' Words

Across
4. A witch would fly on one of these (10)
7. Party decorations (8)

Down
1. The sound an owl makes (4)
2. Visit this place to see animals (3)
3. You learn here (6)
5. You can see this at night (4)
6. The top of a house (4)
7. A type of monkey (6)

'or' Words

puzzle 2

Across
4. Football, basketball, tennis (5)
5. 30 + 10 = (5)
6. Before the afternoon (7)

Down
1. Not long (5)
2. Helps you to see in the dark (5)
3. Bad weather (5)
4. A knight might have one (5)
5. Knife and ___ (4)

Animal Kingdom

puzzle 3

Across
3. A colourful, talking bird (6)
4. The king of the jungle (4)
7. Known for its laugh (5)
8. Can change its colour (9)

Down
1. Polar, brown or grizzly (4)
2. Eight legs, two pincers, one stinging tail (8)
5. Blue ___, the largest mammal on Earth (5)
6. One hump or two (5)

Around Town

puzzle 4

Across
1. Somewhere to stop for a snack (4)
5. Cars, buses and bikes (7)
7. Lots of people (5)
8. You can buy things here (4)
9. Lots of stores in one place (4)

Down
1. Don't forget the popcorn! (6)
2. A place to catch a train (7)
3. You can borrow books here (7)
4. Cars drive on this (4)
6. Learn about history here (6)

What to Wear

puzzle 5

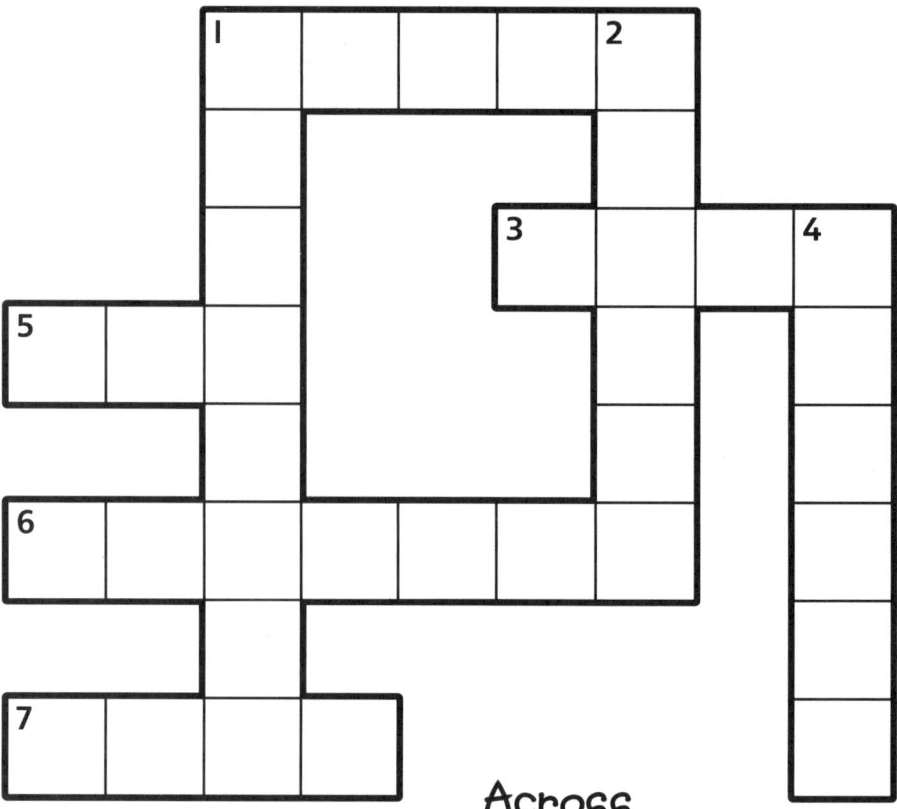

Across
1. Worn inside shoes (5)
3. Keeps you warm outside (4)
5. Protects your head from the sun (3)
6. Usually worn by women and girls (7)
7. Underwear to keep your chest warm (4)

Down
1. Indoor shoes (8)
2. Wear these in warm weather (6)
4. A short-sleeved top (1,5)

Beautiful Blooms

puzzle 6

Across
3. Not a rainflower (9)
5. An arrangement of flowers (7)
7. Tiger ___ was rescued by Peter Pan (4)
8. A bright red wildflower (5)

Down
1. You can make chains with this flower (5)
2. Watch out for this flower's thorns (4)
4. A person who sells flowers (6)
6. The national flower of the Netherlands (5)

Fruit bowl

Across
2. A zesty citrus fruit (5)
5. A fruit you might put in salad (6)
6. The Minions' favourite food (6)
8. A spiky, tropical fruit (9)

Down
1. A large fruit with red flesh and stripy skin (10)
3. A red berry with its seeds on the outside (10)
4. Bunches of these grow on vines (6)
7. A tasty Christmas sauce is made from this fruit (9)

Brilliant Birds

puzzle 8

Across
2. Can be bald or golden (5)
3. Comes out at night (3)
4. A bird of New Zealand (5)
5. Makes holes in trees (10)

Down
1. Pink and stands on one leg (8)
3. The largest bird in the world (7)
6. Has beautiful tail feathers (7)
7. A flightless fast runner from Australia (3)

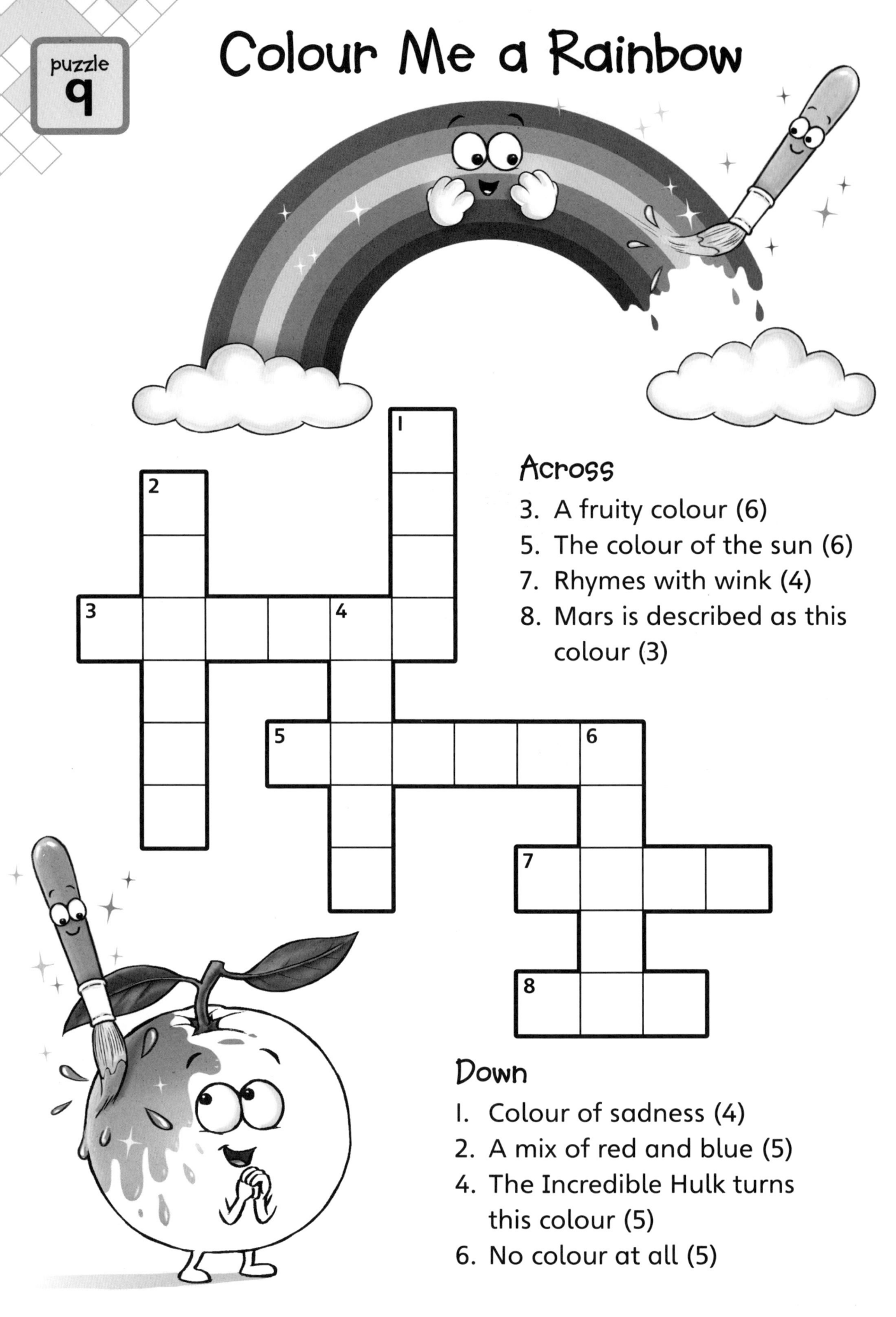

Colour Me a Rainbow

puzzle 9

Across
3. A fruity colour (6)
5. The colour of the sun (6)
7. Rhymes with wink (4)
8. Mars is described as this colour (3)

Down
1. Colour of sadness (4)
2. A mix of red and blue (5)
4. The Incredible Hulk turns this colour (5)
6. No colour at all (5)

Computer Kit

puzzle 10

Across
2. Surf this for information (8)
3. Handheld computer (6)
4. ROM and RAM are types of this (6)
6. For typing – or playing music! (8)
7. Instructions for a computer (4)

Down
1. Also means to 'watch' or 'observe' (7)
2. Don't worry, it won't nibble your cheese! (5)
5. Not a desktop (6)

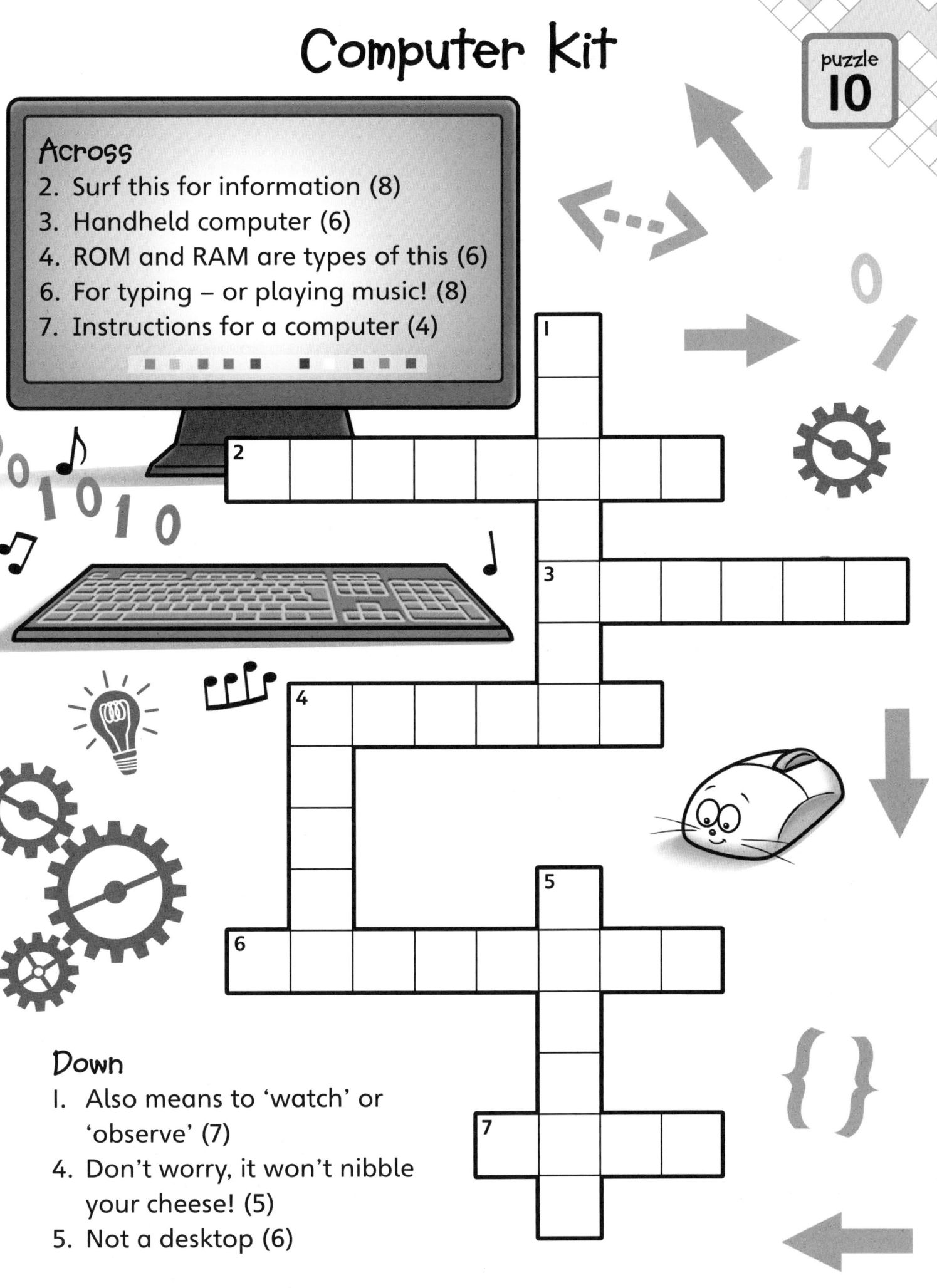

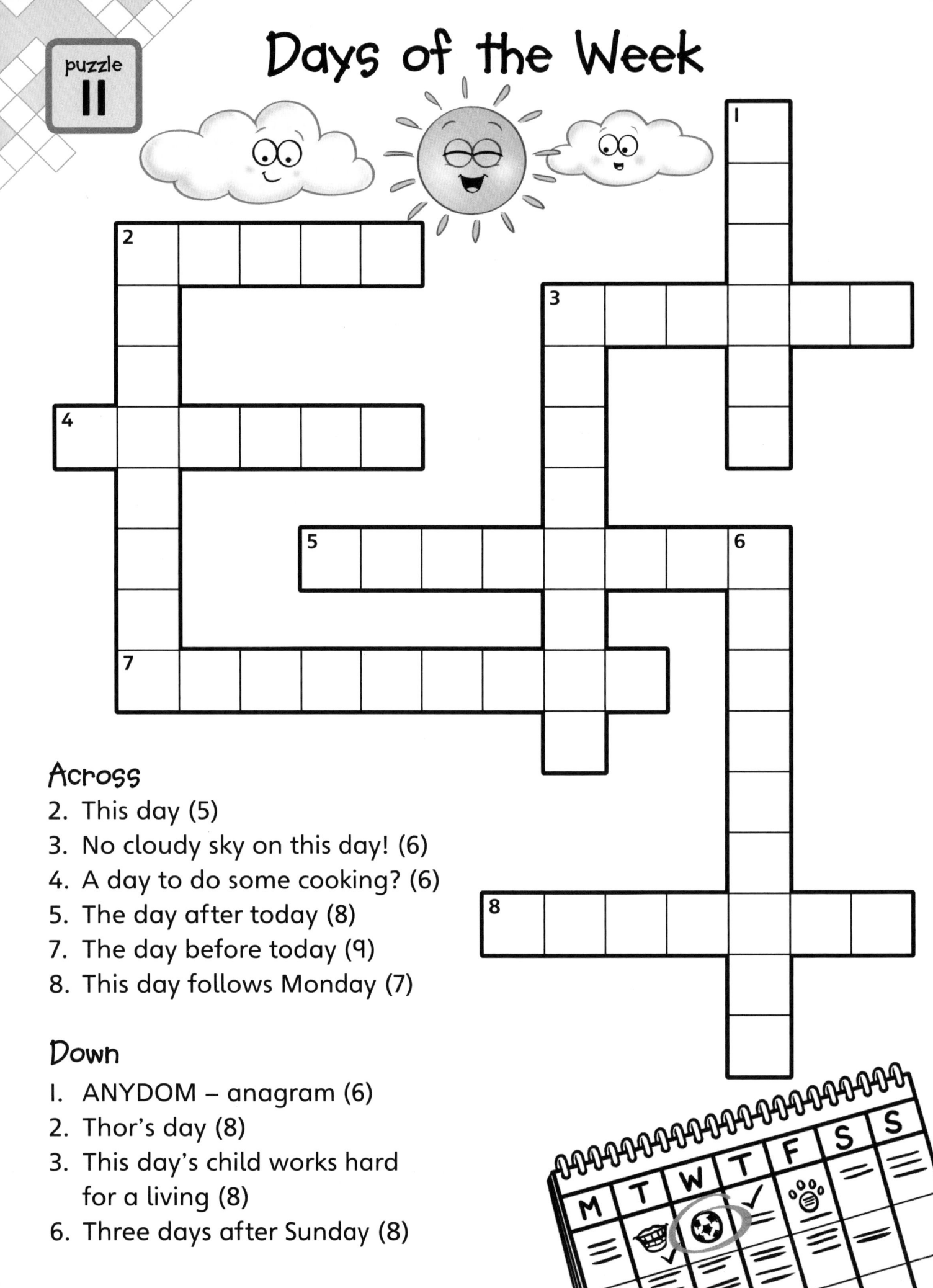

Deep in the Rainforest

puzzle 12

Across

1. This sleepy creature moves slowly (5)
3. ___ dart frog (6)
6. These look like large guinea pigs (8)
7. A spotted big cat (6)
8. The world's biggest rainforest (6)

Down

2. A bird with a large, colourful beak (6)
4. Large ape with orange hair (9)
5. A python or anaconda, for example (5)

Family Tree

puzzle 13

Across
1. Your mother's mother (7)
5. A female sibling (6)
6. The father of one of your parents (7)
8. A male parent (6)

Down
2. A female parent (6)
3. Your aunt or uncle's child (6)
4. A male sibling (7)
7. Your mother's sister (4)

Farm

puzzle 14

Across
1. Surrounds a field (5)
4. A farm vehicle (7)
5. To prepare a field for planting crops (6)
7. Where a horse lives (6)

Down
1. The woolly coat of a sheep (6)
2. Where produce is sold (6)
3. Where crops grow (5)
4. Animals drink from this (6)
6. A group of cows (4)
8. A farm buiding (4)

Favourite Subjects

puzzle 15

Across
4. Stories and writing (7)
6. Take to the stage (5)
7. The study of the world around us (7)
8. A look at the past (7)

Down
1. Rhythm and tunes (5)
2. Numerical problems (5)
3. Around the world (9)
5. You play these in PE (7)

Movie Magic

puzzle 16

Across
4. Winnie the Pooh's bouncy friend (6)
5. Elsa's sister (4)
7. Mary ___, a magical nanny (7)

Down
1. There were 101 of these (10)
2. Simba was the *Lion* ___ (4)
3. Merrida was this (5)
6. A fishy tale, *Finding* ___ (4)
7. Buzz, Woody and Bo Peep were part of this (3,5)

puzzle 17

Frightful Fiends

Across
2. A ghost found at the opera? (7)
6. Rest in peace (I,I,I)
7. Another word for a graveyard (8)
8. Dracula sleeps in one of these (6)

Down
1. Undead person (6)
3. Describes a place with ghosts (7)
4. A body of bones (8)
5. Look out for one of these when there is a full Moon! (8)

On Holiday

puzzle 18

Across
2. People on holiday are these (8)
4. You'll pack this (8)
6. You might write and send one to a friend (8)

Down
1. Protects you from the sun (3,6)
3. You'll need this when going abroad (8)
5. You fly from one of these (7)
7. You might camp in one (4)

Around the House

puzzle 19

Across
3. Rest your head on this (6)
5. Where you cook (7)
6. Scrub-a-dub-dub in the ___ tub (4)
8. Look in this to see who's the fairest of them all (6)

Down
1. A chest of ___ (7)
2. Keeps things chilled (6)
4. Put it in a frame (7)

Playtime Fun

Across
2. Flies in the wind (4)
4. Good for building with (6)
6. Create pictures with these (6)
7. A little toy person to play with (4)

Down
1. You fit the pieces together (6)
3. Choo choo! (5)
5. Play catch with this (4)

Secret Spies

puzzle 21

Across
1. To blend in, spies have to go ___ (10)
4. These shade your eyes (10)
6. Spies try to find out these (7)
8. This needs cracking (4)

Down
2. Wear this to go unnoticed (8)
3. A listening device (3)
5. You'll need a secret one (8)
7. Put things in here to keep them ___ (4)

Let's Celebrate!

puzzle 22

Across
3. A South Asian festival of lights (6)
6. A seven-day Jewish celebration (8)
7. An important Muslim festival (3)
8. Often exchanged at times of celebration (5)

Down
1. Associated with Saint Nicholas and Jesus (9)
2. Lion dances are part of ___ New Year (4)
4. A colourful march or walk during a celebration (6)
5. Vesak (Buddha Day) is celebrated by ___ (9)

Marvellous Maths

puzzle 23

Across
3. Right, acute and obtuse are examples of these (6)
5. Take away (8)
6. Split into groups (6)
8. Helps you check your answers (10)

Down
1. Find out how heavy something is (5)
2. A ruler helps you to do this (7)
4. Times one number by another (8)
7. Geometry is to do with these (6)

Pirates Ahoy!

puzzle 24

Across
4. Robert Louis Stevenson wrote about *Treasure* ___ (6)
5. X marks this (4)
6. You might see a skull and crossbones on this (4)
7. Shiver me ___ (7)

Down
1. Load this to fire at your enemies (6)
2. Pieces of ___ (5)
3. Don't upset the captain, or you might have to walk this (5)
5. Long John ___ (6)

puzzle 25

'Q' Words

Across
2. A journey to find something (5)
4. Four of something (4)
5. Lives in the ocean (5)
6. Not loud (5)
7. Keep your arrows here (6)

Down
1. Water, juice or milk, for example (6)
3. You do this in very bright light (6)
5. A sparkly circle sewn on to clothing (6)
7. A game of questions (5)

Reptiles

Across
3. Roald Dahl wrote about an enormous one (9)
5. Some lizards can lose this to escape danger (4)
6. Baby reptiles hatch from these (4)
7. This very large snake squeezes its prey (6)

Down
1. Reptiles have ___ blood (4)
2. The giant ___ lives on the Galápagos Islands (8)
3. This snake is king (5)
4. Komodo or bearded ___ (6)

Rumble in the Jungle

Across
4. Rudyard ___, author of *The Jungle Book* (7)
5. Jungles are usually found near this imaginary line around the Earth (7)
6. Cities are known as ___ jungles (5)
8. The sound a parrot makes (6)

Down
1. Howler or spider ___ (6)
2. Use these to spot faraway jungle creatures (10)
3. A creeping plant (4)
7. A boggy wet part of a jungle (3)

'igh' Words

puzzle 28

Across
5. Not loose (5)
6. Breathe a ___ of relief (4)
7. A dangerous or difficult situation (6)
8. How tall something is (6)

Down
1. A frightening dream (9)
2. Very pleasant (10)
3. The opposite of day (5)
4. Between daylight and darkness (8)

Super Shapes

puzzle 29

Across
2. A regular quadrilateral (6)
3. A twinkly polygon (4)
5. Also a precious gemstone (7)
6. A round shape (6)

Down
1. The Moon can be this shape (8)
4. A shape with three sides (8)

Super Sports

puzzle 30

Across
2. Play this game and you might get a hole-in-one (4)
4. You can raise a racket in this game (6)
6. Wicket-keepers play this (7)
8. The Tour de France is a big race in this sport (7)

Down
1. Can be ice or field (6)
3. Shoot hoops and slam dunk (10)
5. Can be done on the web or ocean (7)
7. You aim to 'try' in this sport (5)

puzzle 31

Verbs

Across
1. ___ a book (4)
4. Rattle or shudder (5)
5. Move through water (4)
6. Communicate verbally (4)

Down
2. Move with rhythm (5)
3. A long jump (4)
4. Run swiftly (6)
5. Speak in a musical way (5)

Transport

puzzle 32

Across
3. Flies using hot air (7)
5. An underwater craft (9)
7. Open this after you jump out of a plane (9)
8. A flat, floating craft (4)

Down
1. Floats on air over water, land or ice (10)
2. Sometimes called a chopper (10)
4. Carries people around town (3)
6. You have to paddle this (5)

Under the Sea

puzzle 33

Across
2. You might think this 'fish' would twinkle (8)
3. Reefs can be made of this (5)
5. This wobbly 'fish' can sting (9)
7. These walk sideways (5)
8. This type of seaweed creates underwater forests (4)

Down
1. Whales eat this (8)
4. Has two large claws (7)
6. You might find a pearl inside this (6)

When I Grow Up...

puzzle **34**

Across
1. Someone who helps poorly animals (3)
3. See one when you're ill (6)
4. Might work in a laboratory (9)
6. Cooks tasty meals (4)
7. Grows your food (6)

Down
2. Designs and builds machines (8)
3. Cares for your teeth (7)
5. Helps you to learn (7)

Woodland Animals

puzzle 35

Across
1. Night flyer (3)
3. Buries nuts (8)
5. An insect with hard wing cases (6)
7. Builds dams (6)
8. Fantastic Mr ___ (3)

Down
1. Lives in a sett (6)
2. An elephant might be scared of this (5)
4. Rolls into a spiky ball (8)
6. Can have antlers (4)

'oi' Words

puzzle 36

Across
2. Keep away from someone or something (5)
3. Dangerous substance (6)
4. You put this medicine on your skin (8)
6. Ruin (5)

Down
1. An option (6)
2. A human-like robot (7)
3. Extend your finger, or a sharp end (5)
5. Slightly wet (5)

Favourite Characters

puzzle 37

Across
1. Sherlock Holmes's friend (6)
3. Neverland fairy (6,4)
6. Book-loving girl with powers (7)
7. Bunny cousin of Peter (8)

Down
2. Enid Blyton's Secret ___ (5)
3. He's a tank engine (6)
4. This bear likes marmalade (10)
5. Gamekeeper at Hogwarts (6)

Party Time

puzzle 38

Across
2. Wear a costume to this party (5,5)
3. Celebrating the day you were born (8)
6. Pass the ___ (6)
8. Colourful paper decorations (9)

Down
1. Ask people to come to your party (6)
4. Person in charge of the music (2)
5. Blow these out and make a wish (7)
7. People going to a party (6)

'm' Words

puzzle 40

Across
1. A person – or monster! – wrapped in bandages (5)
4. Wash the floor with this (3)
6. Take this when you're ill (8)
7. Fur around a lion's head (4)

Down
2. Picture made from small stones or tiles (6)
3. Not talk clearly (6)
4. Someone who does magic (8)
5. Everyone loves jumping in ___ puddles (5)
6. Don't get lost in here! (4)

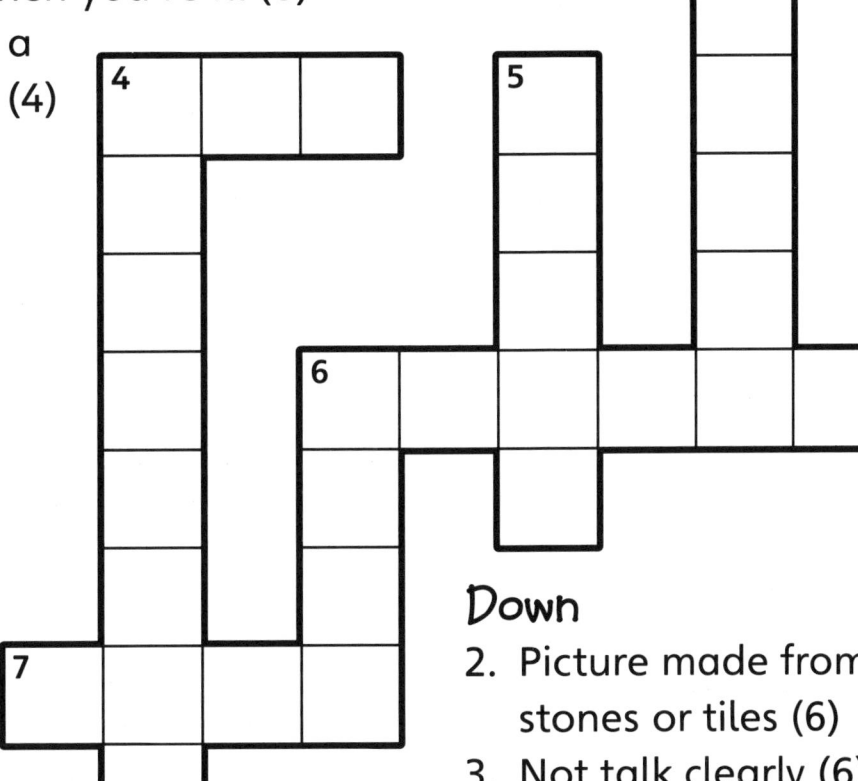

puzzle 41 — In the Library

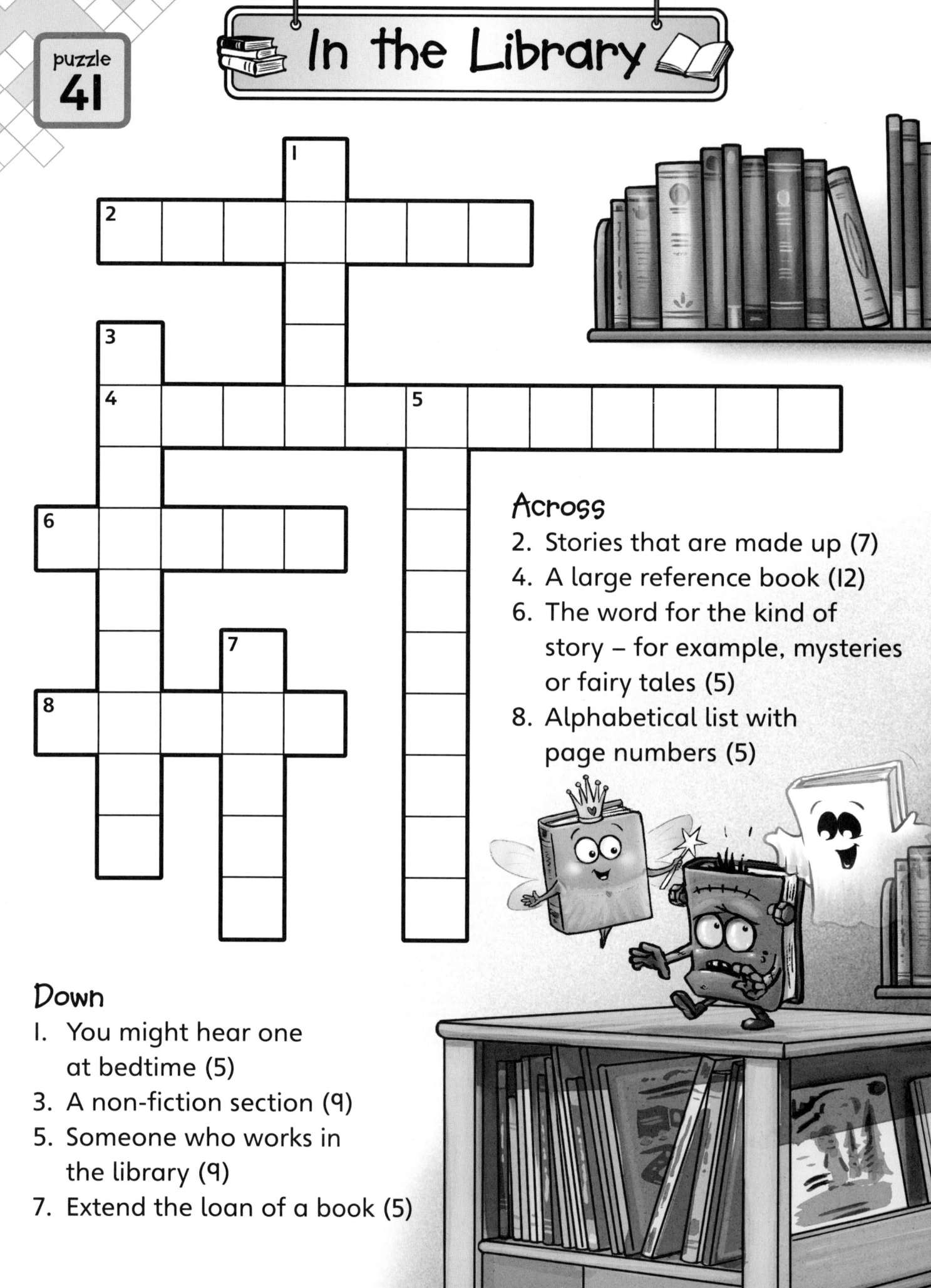

Across
2. Stories that are made up (7)
4. A large reference book (12)
6. The word for the kind of story – for example, mysteries or fairy tales (5)
8. Alphabetical list with page numbers (5)

Down
1. You might hear one at bedtime (5)
3. A non-fiction section (9)
5. Someone who works in the library (9)
7. Extend the loan of a book (5)

At the Gallery

puzzle 42

Across
2. Da Vinci's ___ Lisa (4)
4. A 3D piece of art (9)
5. This holds an artist's canvas while they paint (5)
7. A picture of a person (8)

Down
1. A great work of art (11)
3. Van Gogh's flowers (10)
6. Someone who creates art (6)

puzzle 43

Perfect Pets

Across
3. Pets like to do this with you (4)
4. This shiny pet lives in a tank (8)
5. You might keep a dog here (6)
6. A pet rabbit's home (5)
7. Use this to walk your dog (4)

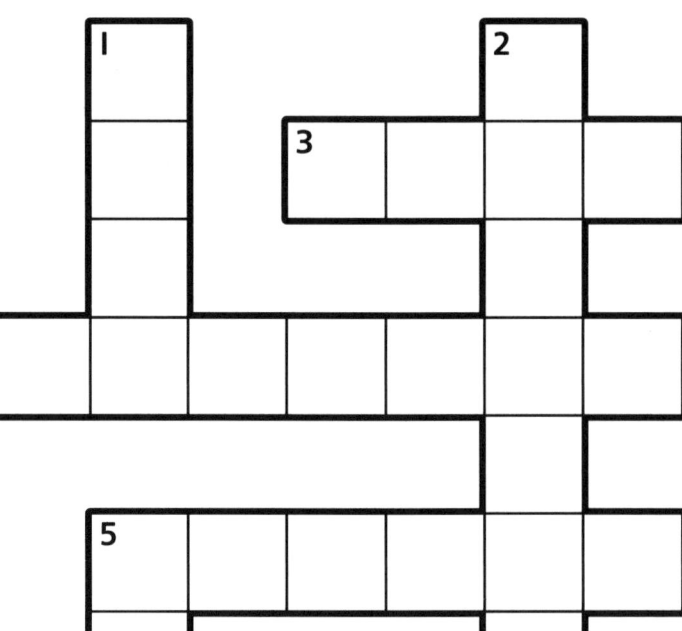

Down
1. Fill this with clean water regularly (4)
2. Small pet that fills its cheeks (7)
5. A baby cat or rabbit (6)

At the Café

puzzle 44

Across
3. Cup___, a baked sweet treat (4)
4. Meal in the middle of the day (5)
6. Like a cake but can be sweet or savoury (6)
7. A flavoured milk drink (9)

Down
1. Slices of bread with a filling in between (8)
2. This hot drink can be made with a bag (3)
5. A hot drink made from beans (6)
8. You might get one with a cold drink (8)

On the Train

puzzle 45

Across
2. Buy this to travel (6)
4. People on a train are these (10)
6. A train runs on this (5)
7. Suitcases and bags (7)

Down
1. List of where and when trains go (9)
3. This is pulled by a locomotive (8)
5. Person who checks your ticket (9)
7. You wait on this (8)

Eating Out

Across
2. A square of cloth or paper to wipe your face or hands (4)
4. A place to go out to eat (10)
7. The sweet course (7)
8. You place this to get your food (5)

Down
1. Salt and ___ (6)
3. List of dishes (4)
5. Extra money given for good food and service (3)
6. Save a table (7)

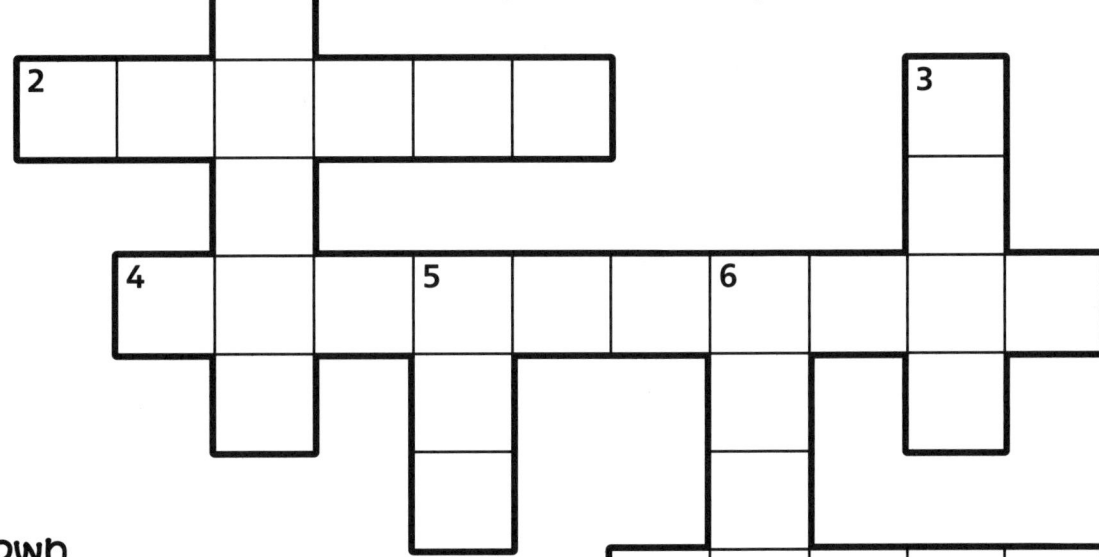

Feeling Social

puzzle 47

Across
2. You think something's funny (1,1,1)
3. A short written phone message (4)
6. A picture to show how you feel (5)
7. Send or show to others (5)

Down
1. A popular website for videos (7)
4. What is a post on Twitter called? (5)
5. A personal blog where you post videos (4)
7. Watch films online (6)

Sweet Treats

puzzle 48

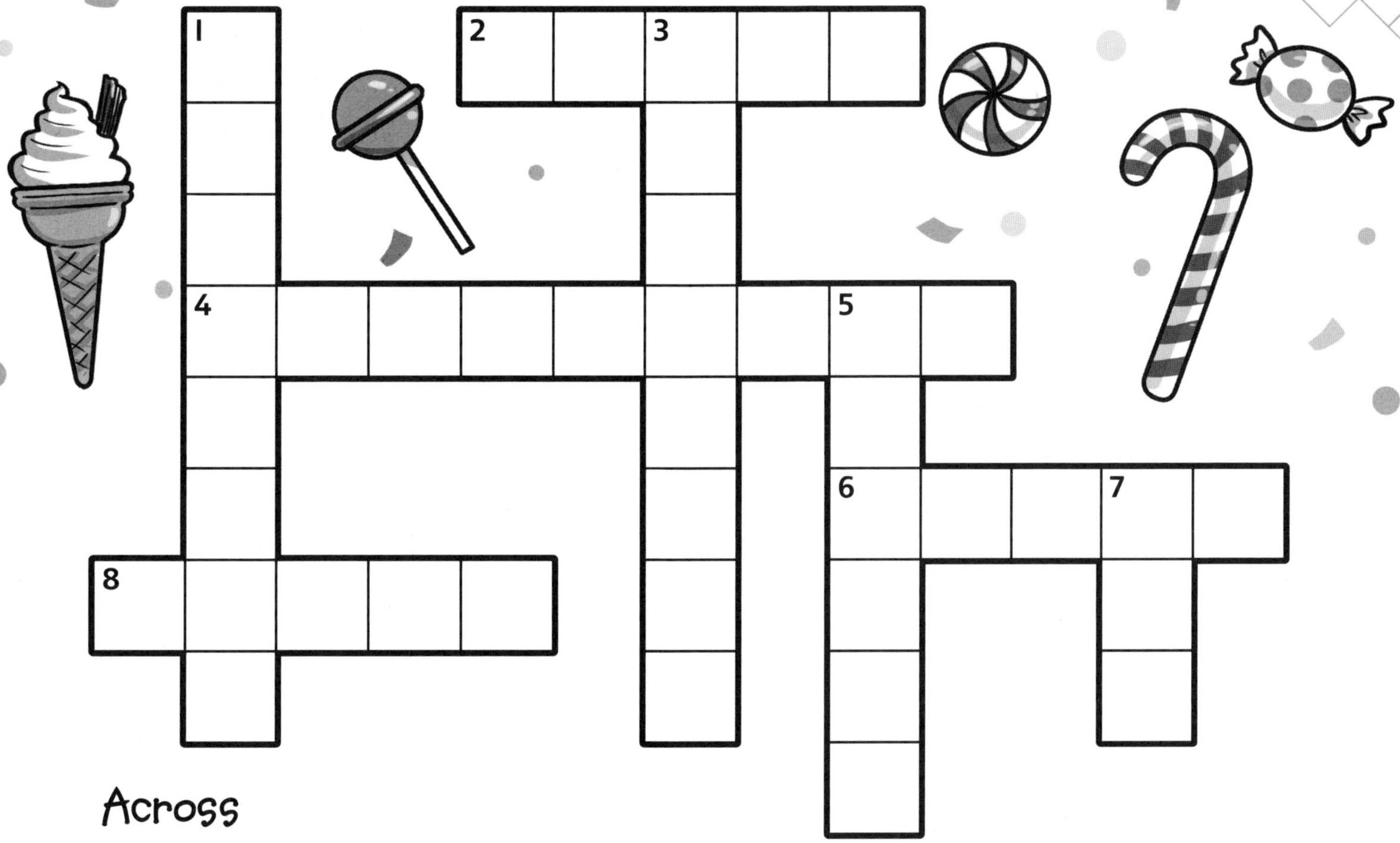

Across
2. These beans come in many colours and flavours (5)
4. Dark, milk or white (9)
6. Harry Potter had chocolate ones (5)
8. Floss, cane or cotton (5)

Down
1. Cold treat on a hot day (3,5)
3. Comes on a stick (8)
5. A hard, chewy sweet (6)
7. Blow bubbles with this (3)

Silent Letters

puzzle 49

Across
3. Truthful (6)
5. Information you've learned (9)
7. A crunchy cookie (7)
8. Not right (5)

'shhh'

Down
1. Captivating, engrossing (11)
2. Not obvious (6)
4. Cut paper with these (8)
6. You have these when you're not sure of something (5)

Homophones

puzzle 50

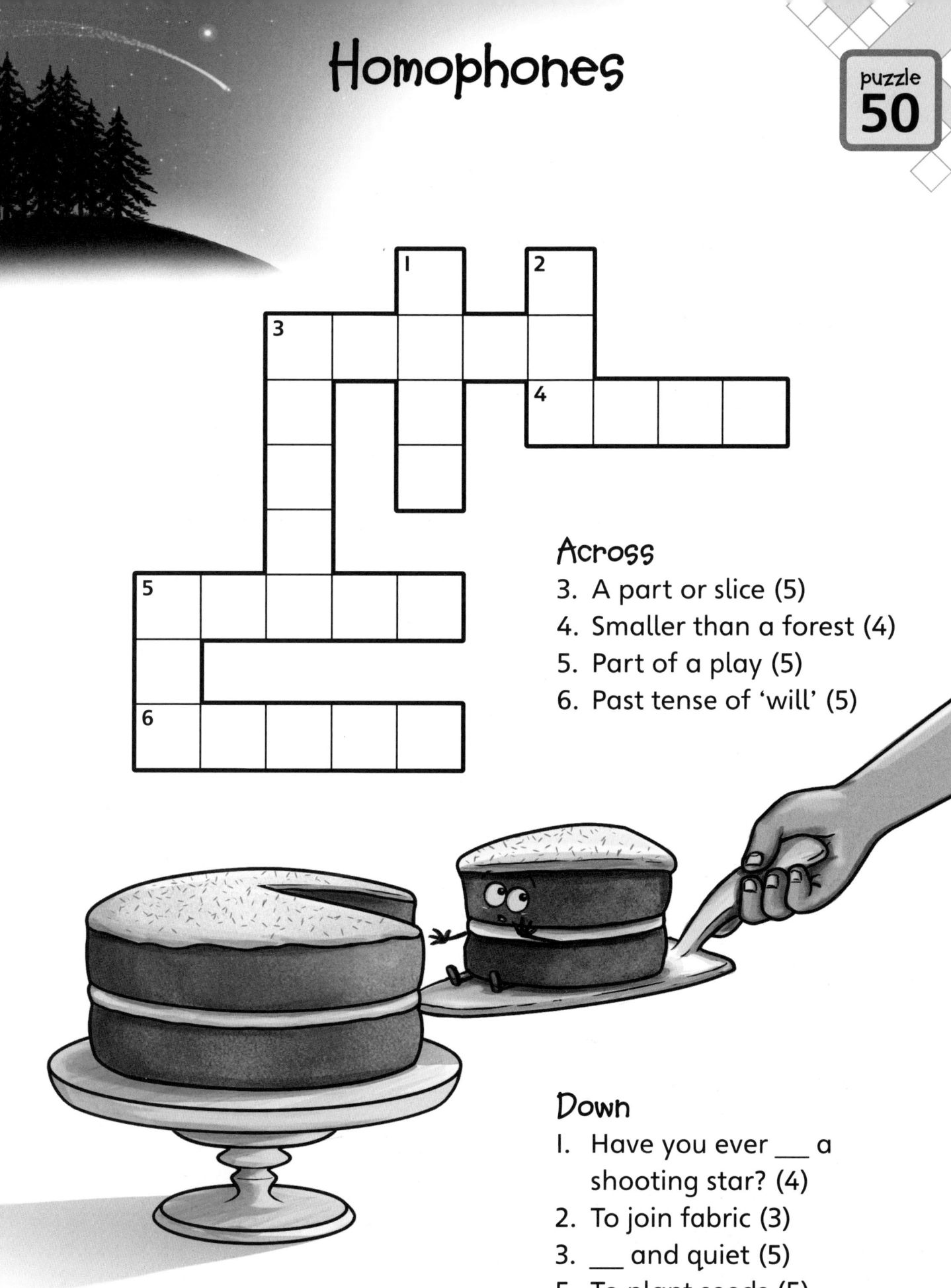

Across
3. A part or slice (5)
4. Smaller than a forest (4)
5. Part of a play (5)
6. Past tense of 'will' (5)

Down
1. Have you ever ___ a shooting star? (4)
2. To join fabric (3)
3. ___ and quiet (5)
5. To plant seeds (5)

Dog Breeds

puzzle 51

Across
2. Which hounds have long ears and short legs? (6)
5. A very common dog breed (8)
7. Snoopy, or Darwin's ship (6)

Down
1. Has dense, curly fur (6)
3. Cocker or springer (7)
4. For example, Jack Russell, Bull, Yorkshire or Boston (7)
6. Could be a featherweight or heavyweight (5)
8. ___ Shepherd (6)

Friends

puzzle 52

Across
1. Your best friend always (1,1,1)
4. A good friend will always ___ to your worries (6)
5. Batman's crime-fighting partner (5)
7. Play___ or team___ (4)
8. Buzz Lightyear's cowboy friend (5)

Down
2. What kind of ship can't sink? (10)
3. A friend you write to (3,3)
6. Another word for a friend (5)

puzzle 53

Opposites

Across
3. Not weak (6)
4. Not short (4)
5. Not lost (5)

Down
1. Not smooth (5)
2. Not easy (4)
3. Not big (5)
4. Not thick (4)
6. Not on (3)

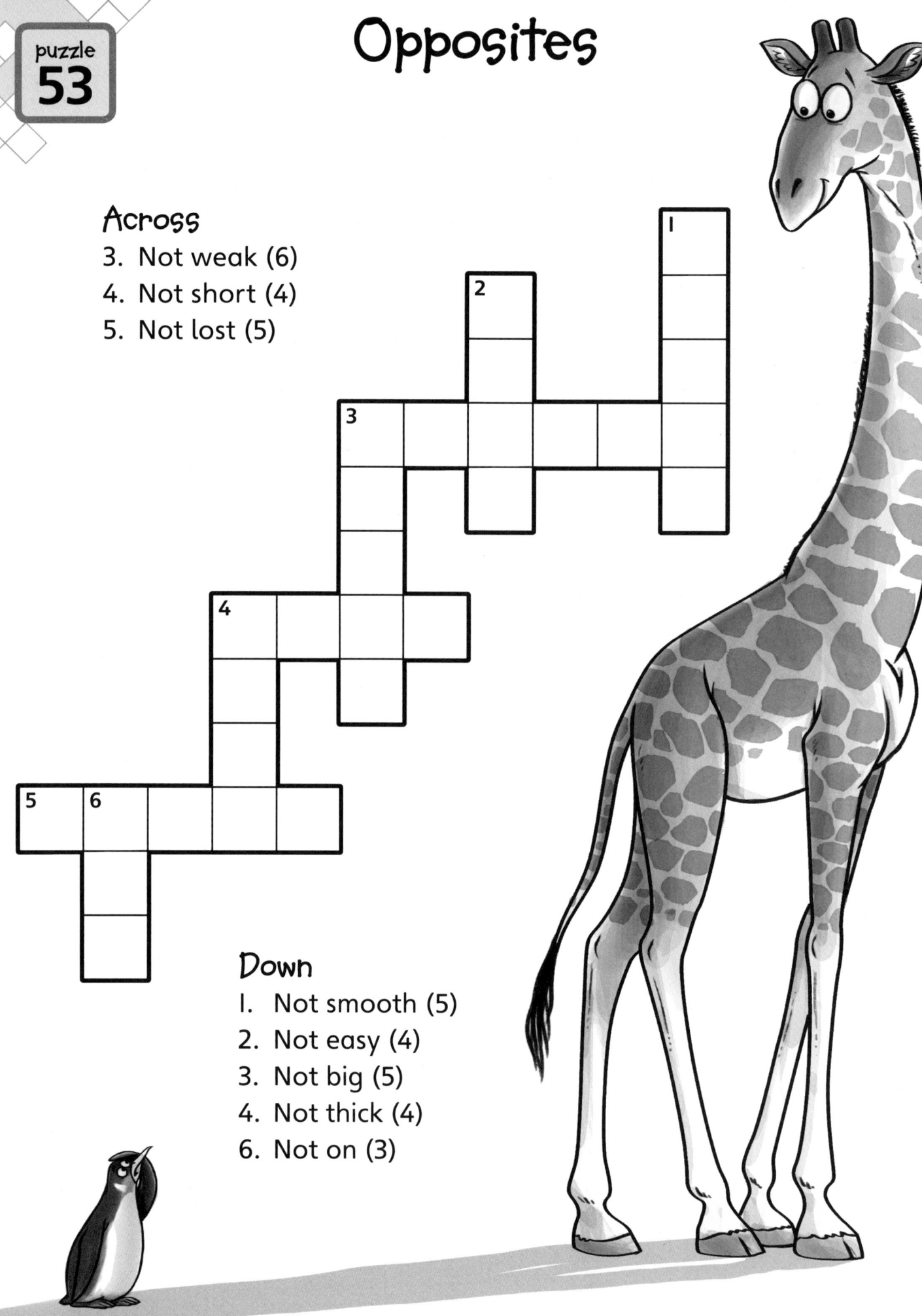

Snow

puzzle 54

Across
3. Throw this in a play fight with friends (8)
5. A sprite associated with winter (4,5)
6. A bank of snow (5)

Down
1. Each one is unique (9)
2. A dome-shaped snow house (5)
3. Usually pulled by horses or reindeer (6)
4. A snowstorm (8)

Brilliant Books

puzzle 55

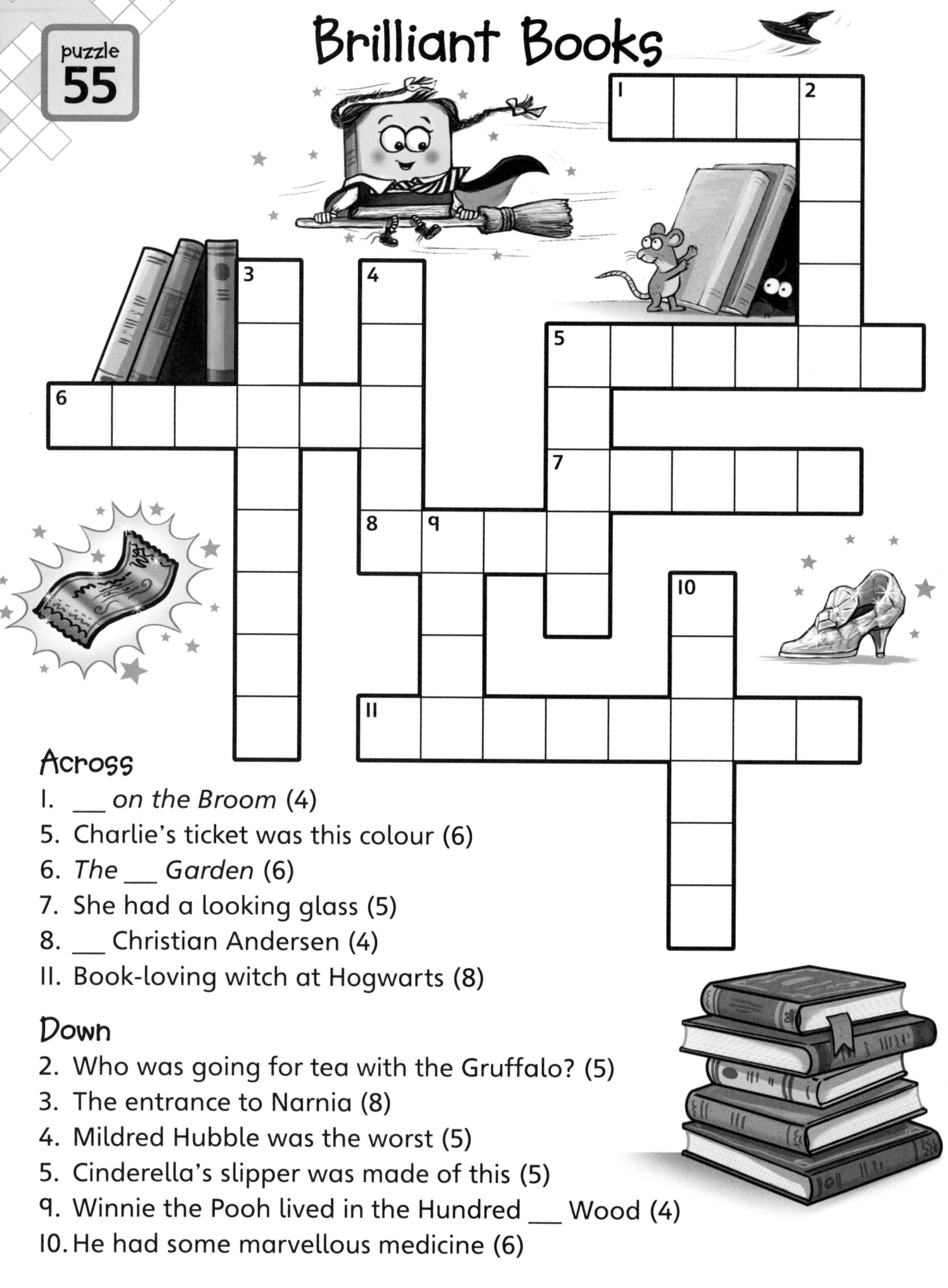

Across
1. ___ on the Broom (4)
5. Charlie's ticket was this colour (6)
6. The ___ Garden (6)
7. She had a looking glass (5)
8. ___ Christian Andersen (4)
11. Book-loving witch at Hogwarts (8)

Down
2. Who was going for tea with the Gruffalo? (5)
3. The entrance to Narnia (8)
4. Mildred Hubble was the worst (5)
5. Cinderella's slipper was made of this (5)
9. Winnie the Pooh lived in the Hundred ___ Wood (4)
10. He had some marvellous medicine (6)

'pt' Words

Across
2. Fascinated (4)
6. Cried (4)
7. Best (7)
8. Appropriate (3)

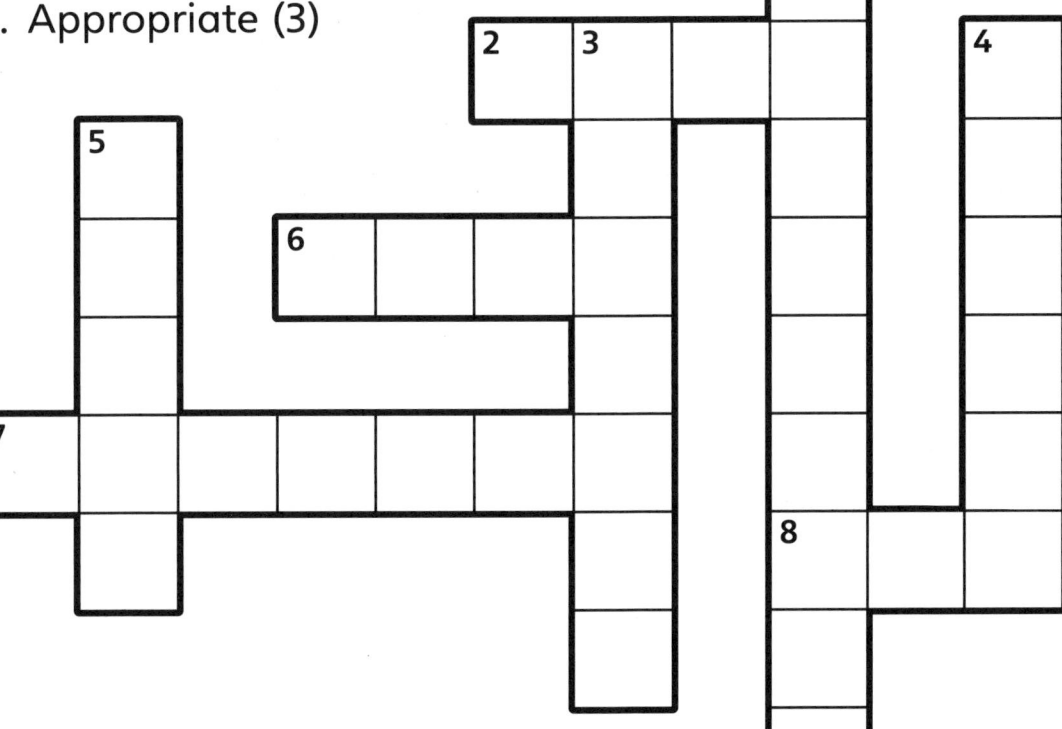

Down
1. A flying cousin of the dinosaurs (11)
3. Try (7)
4. Lines for characters in a play or film (8)
5. Change or modify (5)

puzzle 56